MESSAGES FROM MY HIGHER SELF

MESSAGES FROM MY HIGHER SELF

ROBERT SKUTCH

Cogent Publishing
3770 Barger Street, Unit 604
Shrub Oak NY 10588
cogentpublishing@aol.com

Originally printed in 1982

2 3 4 5 – 23 22 21 20

Dedicated to the Higher Self in each of us.

CONTENTS

Introduction 1
Author's Note 4
On Love 9
On Goals 21
On God 31
A Song 35
On Life 37
On Unity 43
On Truth 47
On Knowledge 51
On Listening 57
On the Ego 63
On Union 67
A Story 71
On Joining 73
On Healing 77
On Identity 81
On Faith 87
On Discovery 91
On Choice 95
A Story 99
On Oneness 101
On Reality 105
On Dreams 111
On the Light 115
On Direction 119
A Story 125
On Recognition 127
On Perception 131
On Mystical Experience 137
On Peace 141
On Remembering 145
A Story 149
On Many Things 151

INTRODUCTION

On a warm summer night in 1972 I watched my husband, Robert Skutch, take a pen and a legal sized pad of yellow lined paper into our darkened living room. "What are you going to do?" I remember asking. I certainly was surprised to hear his answer. "Edgar Cayce said that anyone can do automatic writing, and I'm going to try." This was so out of character for Bob that I eagerly awaited the result. It wasn't long in coming. About a half hour later he ambled into our bedroom and tossed a page full of meaningless squiggles onto my lap. "Nothing," he remarked, "nothing at all."

This was the beginning of Bob's persistent, yet relaxed, approach to a search for the "inner voice." And it took only a few more evenings of sitting with his yellow pad before he began to "hear." It soon became apparent to me that Bob had a definite knack for "listening," and what you will read in this collection is only a fraction of the communications he received from his "higher self."

Watching the process became for me as powerful an experience as reading the writings themselves. The words that flowed from Bob's pen truly did not reflect either his belief system at the time or his style of writing. There was no doubt in my mind that this man I knew so well had touched a part of himself that he had never before revealed to either himself or me.

As the writings unfolded, an entire philosophy began to emerge. Each night I looked forward to yet another inspirational insight, and the excitement of every new message was akin to unwrapping a wondrous gift. The early pages were filled with personal advice which could be followed and tested.

The results were always positive. I particularly remember the first public conference on "New Dimensions in Healing" that our Foundation for Parasensory Investigation underwrote and sponsored in May 1973. We had leased a large auditorium in New York City — the prestigious Alice Tulley Hall at Lincoln Center — to present a rostrum of speakers for the day. Although we had informed many interested people of the event through direct mail, we could not afford paid advertising in the media. The week before the conference I was very discouraged by a pre-registration figure I felt was much too small. I was worried that the hall would be mostly empty, that the excellent speakers would be dissatisfied and that I would be terribly embarrassed. Bob handed me his note pad the night I was most depressed and I read, "Tell Judy that her anxiety is counterproductive to her efforts. Alice Tulley Hall will be filled on Saturday. Every seat will be taken." I grumbled in despair. There were only five days left until the conference, and we had pre-sold only 308 tickets. The auditorium held 1180 seats! I spent the following day just as nervously and once again Bob took down, "Tell Judy that her anxiety is still counter productive to her efforts. The room will be filled." This was a promise to be taken on faith, and so I tried a lesson in trust. The day before the event, one of our friends who worked for a major New York newspaper, telephoned me to tell of her amazement at a "miracle" that had occurred. She had submitted an article as a news item which described the conference in great detail, and her editor had accepted the article and was printing it in that evening's edition. This, she explained, was totally without precedent as articles describing events that were about to take place were "never" printed because they could be construed as being advertising and not news.

The shining spring morning of the conference dawned, and we were amazed and heartened to find a seemingly limitless line of folk waiting for the box office to open. By 10:00 AM we were sold out, and that enormous hall was filled with a glorious light that cannot be described.

Such was the impact of Bob's attunement to his "inner voice;" I grew in awareness with him. So numerous are the tales to tell that I feel a sense of frustration at being limited to a short introduction.

As time passed and the writings continued, I found that each subsequent paragraph of guidance enlarged our appreciation of the internal teacher and increased our faith in our ability to turn within to hear. On May 29, 1975 when I was introduced to the manuscript entitled "A Course in Miracles" and was told of its inception by the pair of psychologists who "scribed" the material, I felt a strong familiarity with that process of "listening" and a profound recognition of its spiritual content. As I read the words of the Course which I would gradually come to know so well, I realized how infinitely grateful I was to Bob for having prepared me to receive my next step.

"A Course in Miracles" describes two types of messengers. "An earthly messenger is not the one who writes the message he delivers. An earthly messenger fulfills his role by giving all his messages away. The messengers of God perform their part by first accepting His messages as for themselves, and then show they understand the messages by giving them away." I know that the following messages received by Bob and given you by him will be recognized as messages from your higher self as well.

Judith Skutch
January, 1982

AUTHOR'S NOTE

The messages in this volume came into being over a four-year period from 1976 through 1979. Although to some it may sound strange, the fact is that I did not really "write" these messages; at least I didn't write them in the traditional sense of the word, and they were certainly not written the way most literary works are. Even though the way the messages were "written" has no real bearing on the messages themselves, I do believe the reader would be interested in knowing how they came to be, for in revealing those details, an important message of its own is revealed: there is a deeper source of wisdom available to *all of us,* one that we can call upon, no matter who we are or what our belief system may be.

My professional literary background consisted primarily of writing original plays for television and radio in the early 1950's. Thereafter my creative writing was devoted to the world of television commercials, and over a fifteen year period more than three hundred of my commercials were produced.

During this time my life was a typical one in that there was a job to go to, a family to support and children to raise. However, the picture did contain one unusual element: one of my children showed signs of having noticeable extrasensory abilities... she appeared to be extremely clairvoyant and to have remarkable telepathic sensitivities as well.

Before she became a part of my life, I was oblivious to matters of the paranormal, and it wasn't until my daughter began exhibiting traits I did not understand that I decided to investigate the subject. By then I had left the advertising world, and had taken up a career as a stockbroker and investment adviser.

One of the books I read was the life story of Edgar Cayce, sometimes referred to as "America's greatest psychic." Cayce, who died at the age of 68 in 1945, and who had left school after the seventh grade in order to go to work, had the ability throughout most of his life to bring forth remarkably accurate medical diagnoses while in a state of deep trance. During his lifetime he gave 30,000 of these "readings," helping vast numbers of people deal with illnesses that the traditional medical community had been unable to help.

Of the many other books I read, the ones describing spiritual healing had the most profound effect on me. It seemed to me, from what I was reading, that the healing effect was no more nor less than a willingness on the part of the healer to join completely with the ill person's mind... to feel that person as completely whole and well.

I was fortunate enough, during this time, to come in contact with Dr. Lawrence LeShan, a psychologist who had developed what he felt was a way of teaching people how to be "healers." His theory was based on the joining of minds, and the discipline he used for this was a series of meditations. I took LeShan's workshop, and thereafter spent a good deal of my spare time working with people who had ailments that had not been successfully treated by orthodox medicine. I worked with people whose illnesses ran the gamut — from warts to cancer, while the healing results ranged from the insignificant to the seemingly miraculous. I would never know when a healing might evolve successfully until after it happened, but I suspect that most people whose health improved were those whose attitudes were the most positive about their chances of getting better.

In 1972 I began reading about "automatic writing,"

a process whereby one takes down information without consciously knowing what it is he or she is writing. A number of books have been written this way, many of which turned out to be remarkably accurate portrayals of historical times... eras about which the authors seemingly knew nothing. This, to me, was another indicator that there is, within all of us, a consciousness that can extend beyond the parameters of the human body and which we are able to tap into if the conditions are right. At the time I remember feeling that this "higher consciousness" also may have something to do with healing.

One evening during the spring of 1972 I was glancing at the book titles in our library, which mostly contained books whose subject matter was para psychological. I was looking for something to read, but I did not know what. Some months before, the Association for Research and Enlightenment had sent us what they called the "Black Book," which was a collection of excerpts from the 30,000 health readings that Edgar Cayce had done during his lifetime. I had glanced at the volume when it had arrived, but had not spent more than five minutes with it. That night, however, I pulled the volume from the shelf, and began to flip the pages. I wasn't looking for anything special, but my eye caught the heading "automatic writing." I was surprised to see such a caption, as I had thought the "Black Book" only contained information relating to health readings. There were two short readings on automatic writing, however. The crux of them both was that "anyone can do automatic writing," and that all one needed to do was to sit quietly and have the willingness.

For some reason this immediately appealed to me. And that very evening I decided to see what would happen if I tried. I figured the best way to "sit quietly" was to do one of the LeShan meditations, and though I sat for about a half an hour with pad and pen in hand, nothing happened. Nothing happened the next two nights either. On the fourth night, however, words began to come into my head, one at a time, and I wrote them down. When I read them later, they did not form meaningful sentences at all. This went on for several nights, and then one night, when I read what I had put down, the sentences did begin to have some meaning.

From this beginning there developed, several years later, the messages that make up this book. Although there was never any "thinking" behind any of the writing that I did this way, and I never sat down to write about a particular subject, I nevertheless would not describe the writing process as "automatic" in the sense in which the word is usually used, for I was quite aware of everything I wrote immediately after writing it.

My early "spontaneous" writings had to do with the healing work in which I had involved myself. At a time when I was bewildered and uncertain as to what healing was all about, the messages I received offered me great encouragement, sustenance and even specific directions.

In 1975, a few years after my wife and I had formed a small non-profit foundation to help fund experimental projects in the field of the paranormal, there came into our lives a 1500-page manuscript entitled "A Course in Miracles." This remarkable self-help tool in spiritual psychotherapy was the work of a woman who had received the entire body of material through a form of automatic writing. The work had such an impact on my wife that she felt it had to be published, and since the "scribe" had been guided to entrust my wife with the manuscript, it seemed only natural that our foundation should do the publishing. The philosophy of this three-volume set of books states that there are but two emotions — love, which is God-created and is all encompassing; and love's opposite — fear, which being man-made, is an illusion. The Course also states that God created us as spirit, not as bodies, and as a consequence God created us all perfectly. I have no doubt that the thoughts in many of the messages I received were in some way inspired by the Course's teachings.

There are two reasons why I wanted to share some of my background with you. The first was to make certain that you realized that the person who took down the messages had neither any prior training in the process involved, nor any real interest in spiritual matters at that time. In fact, until 1971, when I had an emotionally powerful experience while visiting a professional psychic, I didn't even believe in God. The second reason relates to the first: the fact that this collection of messages even exists indicates to me that no matter who you are, if you show a willingness to reach your higher consciousness, you can do so no matter how unbelievable it may at first seem to you.

Finally, let me say that the messages in this volume, along with the teachings of "A Course in Miracles" have helped me achieve a peace of mind that a few years ago I would not have thought possible. I hope they help you in the same way.

Robert Skutch
Tiburon, California
January, 1982

On Love

ON LOVE

Bathed in light, one knows the truth about one's self. Bathed in light, one knows there's no such thing as separation. It is this knowledge that supports us and leads us on our way unto the Home we never left in truth. There are, of course, some other ways of looking at our world, and other ways of thinking what is real and what is of importance, and what is not at all. The pointed truth, however, is that nothing can be real or of importance unless it helps you find real peace and to express true love. All the money in the world can't bring you this; that is an ancient saw. But maybe what is not well known is that there's something that can help you find the peace and love that is within you — as it is within us all. That something is the knowledge that there's nothing that can really matter or mean anything except if it is part of love. What good are things that merely gather dust? What good are fancy foods that turn to waste? What good? But ask what good is love — and you will see the answer in the face of everyone you ask. For they full know what "good" love is. But what they do not know is how to get and keep it. For they constantly look out beyond themselves for it, and it's not there to find. That is the lesson we must learn and teach — that love's within us all... to have, to give, to share. And when we recognize this simple truth, we will no longer need to search for it... except to search ourselves, and it is not that hard to find therein. It merely takes a change of mind, a changed direction from the way you have been taught to think. Would you not want this peace of peace? Then change your way of looking at the world. And then the world will change its way of looking back at you.

ON LOVE

The bells of love have sounded since the birth of God. They have not ceased; they never have forgotten how to ring. However, you must listen if you want to hear. And when you do then others hear as well, because the sound of love is universal. It can't be killed, for who can kill what is immortal? The sense of love is sensed by all, and only needs the curtains parted to reveal itself. Why hold the curtains back when all are waiting to be part of love? But still we hesitate, for we don't know we know. And that is why the light must always be held high. To show the eternality of feelings that are meant to save us from our made-up selves. Don't be afraid. Just wear your love for all to see, and when they do they'll see there's not a single thing to fear, and they shall carry forth the light to others and so on to others and so back to God again.

ON LOVE

Forget the times you think you heard or felt attack upon yourself, and you'll forget what never did occur to your true Self. Forgive your brother who in his insanity has seen you as a separate being, and who does not seem aware of true reality. For when the time is right for him to know the truth then he'll reveal it to himself and through himself. But there's no way one can reveal this to another; one has to find it by oneself. That's why the only help that you can give your brother and your sister is by demonstration... both by word and act. For you can let the world know by your words and deeds what law the universe is based upon — the law of all is based on love. And from that knowledge all will grow to feel, and act upon, the oneness that is our inheritance. And then "attack" will never be perceived again.

ON LOVE

Loneliness is unavoidable to those who have invested other bodies with the golden fruit of love, for then without that fruit they starve. And yet if they could only see that their real selves are blessed with that same fruit, then "loneliness" would never be a word. How simple life can be when we're aware that God has given *all* of us the golden fruit of love. And when you know you have such fruit to offer others in your world, then you will know that you yourself are ever whole and holy... filled with love for you and all who come to share your wealth, as you share theirs. For all the fruit within the bowl comes from the only tree there is — the tree of love called God.

ON LOVE

Your heart is filled with tender thoughts of flowers and of herbs; your heart is full of music that remains a part of all; your heart is God, and if you open up the portals that allow the flowers and the herbs and music to flow forth to all the world, your heart will grow and thus encompass everything you touch. There is no limit to the reach of love, and when you open up the iron gates that you have made you then will throw away the key forever. For the all-embracing heart of God can know no limits once it is released. Nor will you want to smother it again. For there within your heart you have the means of touching all the world, and when you do the world will touch you back. Is this not really what you want? Then open up the gates — there are no dragons there in wait for you. The fields are green, the flowers radiant in their rainbow dress, and all your brothers wait for you to enter and assist them to unlock their gates as well.

ON LOVE

Love is the light that joins the world. Love is the sense of oneness that ensures salvation of yourself and of the world. There is no way that love can be denied, for love is not a part of you, but rather love is all of you. Deny that one is love, and you deny the creativity of God, for love is God's true essence, and in His creation He engulfs you with His love. The presence of love is the basis for healing the world. To remove oneself from the unloving world that one has made, it is but necessary to eliminate the blocks that one has built to hide the presence of the love that lives within us all. It only takes a firm commitment to do thus, and it will then be done. Commitment though means absolute. And at all times. And that is where our ego selves will balk. But that need not deter you, for when you decide, you'll find the gates to Heaven open wide.

ON TRUE LOVE

True love is the realization that there is but one heart and one soul in the universe, and that the beating of that heart is the beating of all hearts. True love means that you do accept the world as one and that you give to all the same way. There can be no disappointments in true love, for there can be no expectations; there can only be complete acceptance at all time. When there is this feeling then there is the feeling of a peace that is complete inside of you. For to accept all souls as one is to accept yourself as well. And therein lies the secret of the joy and beauty one can feel in those relationships that one will choose to have.

ON TRUE LOVE

True love is the realization that there is but one heart and one soul in the universe, and that the beating of that heart is the beating of all hearts. True love means that you do accept the world as one and that you give to all the same way. There can be no disappointments in true love, for there can be no expectations; there can only be complete acceptance at all time. When there is this feeling then there is the feeling of a peace that is complete inside of you. For to accept all souls as one is to accept yourself as well. And therein lies the secret of the joy and beauty one can feel in those relationships that one will choose to have.

ON TRUE LOVE

Peace is where your heart is; your heart is where God is; and God is in us all, because we all are part of God. Feelings of love are but feelings of God, for God is only love. And when we set our ego thoughts aside, there's nothing left but pure God-love, the only kind of love that's real. Don't think that ego-love, love based on our perceptions of another, is the form of love you truly seek. Your ego self may think you so believe, but when you know God-love, you know that any other feeling is a thin and sad attempt to emulate true love. There is no need for emulation when the bona fide is yours inherently. Accept it; know it's yours and you can find it in an instant. Find it, and you'll never have another fear again, for God-love is complete unto itself, there being nothing more. You thought, of course, there could be more, and now you've built a dream so thick with layers of nightmarish covers that to find your true self must appear to be an almost near impossibility. And yet it can be done, and is done every day by those who are aware that they can find the love that is their mark.

ON THE LIGHT OF LOVE

When you touch the light of love you touch the only knowledge of one's self. There is no knowledge but love-knowledge, for that is all that's real, and that is all that knowledge ever means: totality of union, totality of being, totality of feeling. Do not be put aside by words that jar the ego; the "light of love" is just a symbol, as are words of any kind. The only thing that matters is the feelings that you strive to find, so you can once again live as you did, and as you will again. For only by your being cognizant at all times of your goal, can this occur as normally as you now breathe. For once you've dealt with all the layers of the guilt that cover up the light of love, then will you recognize the truths that you have hidden from yourself, and which then will just be. Thus will the light of love be once again revealed, to then shine everywhere and once again be known.

On Goals

ON GOALS

In a garden seen amidst a stretched out plane of green complete with dotted shrubs, bestirs the place of unity: unity of purpose, unity of thought and unity of knowledge of Who we are. Life in this garden is the goal of all who seek to find the peace they know is theirs. And so to this oasis here among the vibrancy of nature are you led to come, for only then will you be ready to experience the garden that is God. Words can't describe the unity that's born here in the hearts of all who come, and yet there is a single purpose for the ones who do remain. The purpose is to nourish flowers in the garden, and thus to help them spread beyond the garden gates, out to the living green that has been nourished for all time and is just waiting to be used to help fulfill its function. For as the flowers spread, and as the garden grows, its boundaries extend out further and still further till the time the garden itself is larger and much more important than the world beyond itself.

This is the dream awakened, the dream that never was. The garden is not just for those few souls who find its peace and harmony a part of all they ever could perceive. The garden is for everyone for all eventually must recognize they can't avoid the beauty and the peace that constantly is beckoning.

Remember then, that peace and love and oneness are not things that d reamers only hope for. They are in truth available to anyone who opts to change directions and direct oneself unto the ever growing garden that is Home. You need but step inside the gates and you are welcome there. And what is best that you'll find the entrance just around the corm from wherever you now dwell.

ON GOALS

The river stretches through the sloping craggy walls of earth and rock, and points its way out to the open sea. And there a single sail is floating midst the barely lifted breeze. "Who sails that ship?" we ask, and when the voice returns we know we have become the boat itself, as well, of course, as all the sea around us, and the helmsman and the crew. The boat of life sails on in search of what it never left. And on the way it takes on many different forms of cargo and of crew. The rudder seems to turn, but as we steer, the ship stays on the only course it knows, no matter how we try to change the way we think we want to go. The course is set; there is not one thing you can do to change it. And blessed are you to touch that knowledge, for you cannot find the port you want except by holding fast to every thought that would oppose, and then releasing them for good. The ship, the fish, the sea are all the same. And so you head for Home.

ON GOALS

The goal of all is all the same... to find the peace and Joy of Home again. What else would be the purpose of our breathing life into a body, but to use that body in a way that best serves God. And by our "serving" we but mean to merely recognize that we are all the children of our Father, and when we realize that we are one, then can we know that love is but the one emotion that there ever was or is. And in that knowledge will the peace of God prevail and thus pervade each breath that each of us will ever take. How can there be another goal than this when everything but love is merely dust that scatters to the winds.

What meaning can the meaningless then have? Let go of all that once seemed vital to your goals, for all your goals are yesterdays, while love is the eternal. When you have recognized the truth of all of this that has been said, then you will know what goal is real, and you will never stray again to try to find your happiness in dust.

ON GOALS

Where do we go from here? How can God's child go anywhere, if in truth one cannot leave, and therefore one has never really left? One only can remain and be. This is what God wants you to know — to recognize within your deepest self that you have never left that which you are, and knowing you have never left, you will re-focus vision so you can observe the truth. If all this seems impractical, then ask yourself what do I want; and if you want to know the peace and joy of God, it will be yours to have by simply waking up. There is no basic difficulty to this seeming problem that you have. The thoughts are there; the only thing that's missing is the faith and willingness you need to see them through. Relax and feel the love of God pour through your every cell when you have given up all thoughts of *this* world, and simply tried to "be." There is an ecstasy unknown within your world, but known forever in the world you never left. So make the choice, and make the one commitment that you need to find your Self and all the peace that unity implies. There is no other answer to your quest.

ON REACHING ONE'S GOAL

What is forgiveness but the chance to show your brothers that we all are one. And in so doing, make the world we know a place more closely allied to the place that is our goal. Don't worry that the goal seems far away. What seems a million miles away can still be reached in just a footstep when the right directions are quite clear. There is no need to wonder how it all can happen once again the way it once had been. No need to worry over things like that, for in so doing you but put a barrier between yourself and your one goal. Just let it happen as it will one day. Work at removing barriers to love, and you will know the bridge will manifest. But first you must let go and love. And in that way all others will begin to do the same. And all will then be one. And one will then be all.

ON GOALS

What is our goal? To "see" the best in everyone we meet. Only in this way can you become at one with the universe. No need to think of *being* best, for we all *are* the best. But this, not many know. And yet it's possible to recognize exactly Who we are. And so to say what one's goal really is, you need but look into your heart, and you will know. It seems a long, long journey, but there's beautiful clear light you will approach at journey's end. And at the end is the beginning, and that's the beauty of the journey you are on.

ON GOALS

Your goal is the goal of all souls... the destiny of past and future melding into one. And so the goal is met. There can't be distance in between the memories of long ago and far ahead, for nothing separates the two, since separation merely is a state of mind. Your goal then is exhibiting the lack of separateness, for in so doing you do join with God, and in that joining there is perfect joy. Yes, God's the One Who puts the joy in joining. And when you are able to express the feeling that is oneness with your brothers — when you actually can feel that oneness, then you'll feel the joy of being... the true and total joy to which we all are heirs. But you must actively participate in feeling this, and then permit the feeling to roll around inside your heart while you do savor it and know its full potential. And then you'll know true joy — and you will know the meaning of your goal... the goal that has indeed been met.

ON GOALS

L onging for the return of the feeling one has had in one's experience — through meditation or spontaneously... longing for the feeling of all knowingness, and of oneness, and of the overall sense of peace and tranquility. Longing for it, because you know it exists for you to experience. And yet it's hard to reach for the experience at will. And that's the sadness of the thought. But it may also be the blessing. For to know that it is there, but to not be able to achieve it easily, may be the answer to why life goes on this way. Struggling to reach that answer — knowing it is there — makes that struggle much more meaningful. And when we touch it once again, even for the briefest flash, we then are sure it's real. That's why we keep on striving for it, for we know when we achieve it once again we will be that much closer to enjoying it forever.

On God

ON GOD

I f what God is were clear to you, then you would have a clearer picture of the true relationship God has with you. God is but love. As simple as that. To tell this yet again is only so the knowledge may be reinforced, for there is just one way the concept can be learned, and that is by repeating and repeating it. And in that way the knowledge spreads, and then the time that's needed to attain true knowledge is compressed. And that is the real goal: to shorten all the time it takes to have your brothers and your sisters know that God is love. For in that knowledge is the only way the unity of humankind can be attained.

ON GROWING TO GOD

Growing to God is the only real goal in your life. What can you name that can compare to all the joy and purposefulness such a goal provides? When one expands one's consciousness to reach to spaces one has never realized were there, then one can better understand and be aware of that which is not only open to us, but which actually resides inside of us, so we can take a hold of it and be a part of it as well. Growing toward God is discovering Who it is you really are — the you that never left your true Creator. It's all there for you to find again. And you can *know* it's there by feeling all the calm and peace of meditation when you do forget the world you've made. This is the message that is told again and yet again. If you but keep it in your mind when cause of conflict shows itself, you will remember Who you are, and you'll forget the rest.

ON QUESTIONING GOD

Wondering about the laws — the so-called laws — of God is a useless exercise. There are no laws of God; there is just God, and the all-encompassing love of God. Why would a force of such completeness — of such perfection — of such absolute positiveness, need any laws. Laws are only to control, and God has not the need to have controls. For all that is of God has always been of God, and will forever be. That's why there is no need for laws, for God just is. Forget the intellectualism egos try to use to rationalize the world of God. God has no intellect and God has need of none. That's why some questions that seem difficult, seem also hard to answer. Yet they are difficult but on your level of belief and on your level of awareness, not on anybody else's. The game is only played out to perfection when it's played by "rules" of God's creation, not be rules the ego's made. Believe in your return to God, and you will have no further reason to become involved with questions of that kind.

A Song

A SONG

Take me to the light. Take me to the depth of all encompassing forgiveness where the unity of purpose surrounds each single mote. Take me to the wondrous knowledge that instills in all of us the grace of God eternal and forever. For that is where the joy that is forever is reality. There are no other ways to know the depth of knowledge. There are no other ways to true eternal love. There are no other ways to celebrate the vastness of the oneness that is truly our inheritance. Take me by the hand and let me see and feel the joy of joys, the love of loves, the truth of truths, that there may be no doubt again in mine or any other mind. For without doubts, one lives the life that was our birth and our eternal selves. There is a vast and growing beauty to be seen and felt and it is there for all to touch. Reach out, and you can taste the miracle of love with true acceptance and you'll never want for more. Ask and seek and when you touch the tenderness of time that never was, you'll never be the same.

On Life

ON LIFE

Suppose the night were never over,
And the day had no surcease.
Suppose the end had no arrival,
And the start had no release.
Suppose the rain would never fall,
And there were never clouds at all.
And what if you were I and I were you,
And we were one forever too.
Suppose that all we saw we didn't see,
And sounds were never known to be.
And songs you sang were never sung,
And bells you heard had never rung.
You'd think if all these things were so,
The world you know would be a dream—
And that, my friend, is not a lie.
For that is why we never "live,"
And why in fact we never die.

ON LIFE

Tell me the secret of life everlasting;
Tell me the secret of joy the eternal;
Tell me what means can be used to reach out toward
The furthest and brightest of stars.
Tell me how long must a person be wary;
Tell me how strong is the Voice from within;
Listen, my child, and you'll know all the answers,
All the things you could imagine there are.
For deep in the heart of your heart is your being,
The spirit and soul that is all of your life.
Reach for that spirit — it's yours and it's of you;
Take it and cherish it with all your might.
For love is the answer to all of your questions;
Love is the goal that all of us seek;
Reach for it, stay with it, hold it forever,
And you will know God every breath, every sight.

ON LIFE AND KNOWLEDGE

Seated by the road of life I wonder at what passes by. I seem to have a longing to perceive the caravan of truth. And all the while the restless and the tired slog their weary way along to nowhere. And yet I sit and watch. Un-sorrowed. For I am now aware the seeming wretched *are* upon their way, though they do not at this time seem to know it. It is a joyful sight then that I see, knowing how they will appear when they first turn the bend ahead and see what is in store for them. And as they pass there are among them mirrors of light dancing lithely on their way. They go the same direction, but the difference is that one has knowledge and will seem to get there more directly than the rest. At last, I have watched long enough. The long procession will not end, and so I choose to join it. And I know that I as well will mirror light to those who may be watching as was I. The message is of course quite clear; there is no real reality to any moment that we see. The travelers are in truth the same. We see them differently, but they are one — and have one goal. And somewhere when the road runs out of turns, there will the treasure chest of knowledge be at last, and we will all partake. For we will know we never have surrendered up the treasure chest that is our true inheritance.

ON LIFE

There is no death; there's only life that will forever be, though it's not life as now perceived by you. It's life as God would know... life that offers up itself in such a dignity that you can't help but feel that it's the only life that we will ever know. Look upon your life as God's life; look upon your love as God's love, for God's life and God's love are identical. There is no difference; there can be no difference. When you are aware of all the real and ever growing beauty of God love, you never will again think that there's something else that's real. This can't be said too often, for it is the basis of all things we do and feel. If we do good, we're doing God's own work; if we feel good, we're feeling God's own love. How can one constantly remember this? By simply not forgetting Who we are.

On Unity

ON UNITY

Tender is the time when unity is forever joined, for reaching out to comfort all who ever are or ever were is the highest form of giving. Don't be deluded into thinking there are other forms of satisfaction. There is but one form of true joy — the state we all aspire to remember. And that form, as is so apparent, is of love. And what is love you ask? It is the ultimate form of knowledge of Who you are, and of knowing we are all the same and of sensing and sending the shared belief of oneness with us all. There can be no judging when there is true love; there can be no sense of longing or of something lacking. There can only be true identity with the within. Live within, and you will love all those who seem to be beyond the true within. And what else can there be than that totality of Union.

ON UNITY

Watch for signs that tell you with a certainty that's absolute that all is one within the world you see. That all is one in God's world is a truth that needs no reinforcement. But in the world that you inhabit it is also true, though it may not seem so to you. There is no other way that it can be, for what you really are cannot be changed by putting on a masquerade effect. And underneath there always is the one reality that is our true inheritance. Look past the costume... see it not. And you will see the light that shines within us all, the same identity that we have always been. And when you have this knowledge, you'll no longer have the need of self-defense, for you will only see true love, and therefore will extend but love. And that is where we all are seeking to arrive... the state of peace that's born of love.

ON UNITY

L et your brothers know at all times they are you. Do this in whatever way may be appropriate, be it by touch, by word, by look or sense. When you are able to do this, you'll find a joyful union of both mind and spirit too. For all your brothers now are sending this to you or they are waiting you to offer it to them. And once it's offered up it only can be recognized and warmly welcomed in return. The power of love is all encompassing as you well know; so do not hide your love beneath the ego's shroud, for that just makes it harder to fulfill your destiny.

On Truth

ON TRUTH

L ost in a world of alien shapes, the reality of Who you are is hidden from the sunlight that is blanketing the tops of trees. You can't expect to find the winding path that leads you Home when you but wander aimlessly among the giant trees that hide the light of Who you are. And you will stay in darkness and in seeming helplessness as long as you decline to recognize you know the truth of where it is you are, and where it is you're going. It does seem much too frightening to feel there is no path to take, for then what would your purpose be in being there at all. And yet the truth itself provokes no fear at all, because the light of Who you are tells everything about your goal. There is no path, because you're there already, and when you decide to spread the trees to the horizon of your soul, then all the light that ever was will pour down on your world, and you'll be Home.

ON TRUTH

Don't ever try to count the ways of the world before you know your sums. There is but one way of the world. The way of God. Remember, yours is but a speck within the vacuum of time... a meaningless existence that is only given meaning when it's put into perspective. From the point of view of truth, the meaning of your life is challenge — challenge to develop the ideas of oneness. So forget what you believe you've learned, and learn the truth that's buried deep inside you. Know that you and God are One, and One means for forever. Aside from being the one truth there is, this attitude can give the world the torch it needs to ignite the candle of knowledge. And when that happens, then will you realize what the "rules" of the game have really been, and how you have been playing by your own misguided rules. This is important to keep in mind, for it is the basis of your learning what true happiness can be — for you, and for the world.

ON TRUTH AND ILLUSION

The tendency to tell the world that one is not a part of the entire whole is just a policy of self-defense. What purpose does this serve? It cannot nourish your true self, for it is not a statement that is true. But also it cannot support the ego self, because the ego can't in truth receive support at any time, for what can one declare that could in any way make an illusion real? There are two ways to leave the world that you have made. One is to build illusions into such a terrifying state that one cries "help!, no more of this," surrendering in terror to one's real reality; the other is to have the knowledge that the dream is but a dream, and thus decide in peace to waken and rejoice. One way will *have* to happen at some time. Which will you choose?

On Knowledge

ON KNOWLEDGE

When one is still in meditative thought... when one can reach the inner depths of peace and tranquility, then one has knowledge at the tips of one's heart. It is the knowledge of the beauty and the love of God — the beauty and the love that one can feel for all that is around one... people, things and all that one can both imagine and perceive. The depth of knowledge such as that is very real, and when you're there in peace, there's nothing else that does exist except the being of one's feeling one with All. Or one with nothing, for all of our perceptions are but nothing. And so it would depend upon what level you begin approaching the idea. If on the ego level, it is being one with nothing. On the level that is real, however, it is being one with God and all the lights in the entire universe. And as we recognize more fully feelings that are peace and purity and simple oneness, then we know much more completely Who the real I is, and what the I is for. It is to know this peace, and share it and to bring it to the others who will then do just the same. And then when every mind is known as one, will we be Horne and be at peace again.

ON KNOWLEDGE

In the depths of one's consciousness there dwells the knowledge of the truth about reality. This knowledge is within us all, and yet it is so difficult to grasp. Why so? Because the knowledge is locked up inside with such security that it is near impossible to reach. And yet there is a way. And it's available to everyone. All that is needed is persistence and courage. Persistence to keep trying to work toward the goal of reaching it, and courage to keep wanting to. For we're not sure what it would mean to us if we were actually to reach this knowledge without first knowing how it would affect our lives. And so the struggle goes from century to century, because we are afraid to reach for the unknown. But the unknown is the excitement that can make the present seem worth while. And the unknown is really not unknown at all, but is in fact the known. The only real known that there is. For deep within us we do know the truth — that love and brotherhood have always been our natural inheritance, and that we must seek out our inner knowledge so that it can start us — and the world — upon the way to perfect harmony.

ON KNOWLEDGE

When the wind sings loudly and the trees are bending to the sound of Heaven's song, then does the magic of the mystery of life spring forth to hold you in its spell. For deep within the wind there is an element of God that one cannot dispel, that one cannot make separate from self or any other self. Wipe clean your mind at times like these, and you will feel a certainty of God, of love eternal, as you seldom felt before. It is a feeling born of knowledge that the mightiest and tiniest of forces are the same. They each are but a moment in the chronicle of time that of itself has little meaning 'cept as one delves deeper into what such matters really signify. And who can ever say in words what meaning there can be attributed to all that God has ever been? Words cannot ever take the place of knowledge and of feelings that transcend the senses of the body to reveal to you the truth of Who you really are. The sun, the wind, the clouds, they all have different meanings to a million different eyes. But to the only Eye there is, the Eye that offers us such perfect vision, meanings are but one. And when we make the choice at last to say exactly what the meaning is, we have but one small word to say. The word, of course, is "love." For God just is.

ON KNOWLEDGE

Know who you are! Know that you are complete unto yourself because you are a part of everything, and everything is part of you. There never is a need to sacrifice a single thing, for sacrifice is of the mind, and what's complete can never sacrifice. Remember, nothing can be given up from that which stays forever whole. When you believe you're sacrificing, it is not God's child who's feeling that, but that one part of you that would deny exactly Who you are. But when you reach that point of knowledge where you *know* just Who you are, there will be no such thought as sacrifice. And there will be no symbol-words as "suffer," "terror," "loss" or "hate." So recognize that you are perfect, and you'll recognize the true perfection of all things and people that your mind exposes you to see. And then will you "see" nothing and know everything, because a mind that's unified is one that never has left God, and therefore is complete and joined with that which is its Home.

On Listening

ON LISTENING

Listen, listen and know the voice you hear is the one voice of all infinity — the voice of higher being that can help you be that part of you that never left its Home. It is the voice that helps you feel and show the total love of your inheritance. There is no other way to touch the heart of your own being, for all we ever really feel are feelings of real love. Do not disguise the voice you hear, it cannot be disguised. Do not foreclose the voice; it cannot be foreclosed. Do not forsake the voice; it cannot be forsaken. Trust it well, and it will certainly reward both you and all you touch.

ON LISTENING

L isten to your inner voice and hear the way to God. Listen with your Higher Sense, and know the truth, the way to joy. There are no other ways to happy hearts and festive thoughts except the way the real Self knows. Just take the path and then ignore the signposts placed so cunningly within your way, for they point nowhere though it seems they point to everywhere. But "everywhere" is only in one place, and you already happen to be there, though you but know it rarely. When you do, however, there can be no doubt it is your one and only goal. So open up your heart and let it happen to you now. It can; it will; it happens all the time.

ON LISTENING

Said simply, the Voice for God is spoken at all times. Just listen and you'll hear. There is no mind that cannot hear, just as there is no mind that cannot open to the knowledge that the Voice itself is there. And it will answer all your questions, help you find your own direction if you only will allow it to. Be still, be quiet, be at One and you will know you've heard the Voice for God that speaks to you. It is a gift to you, but it is not a gift unless it is accepted first. So don't let your Creator stand with open, empty arms; reach out and take the gift; it's yours and it's awaiting you.

ON FALSE LISTENING

At times when we do seek to learn the truth about ourselves, we find a voice that whispers loudly that there is no truth at all — the voice that says there only is the way you *feel*, and *that's* the only truth. But this is only half the tale as well as half the truth. For when we seek the truth, we have to go beyond that voice, and recognize it's there to keep our selves from finding that we really all are just the same. If one gets deep beyond the surface selves we think we are, one finds a knowledge of perfection... total love that wants not one correction or reward for self or others. For in that deeper inwardness there dwells perfection waiting to be found and recognized. The voice one mostly hears is there to keep you from discovering the heart of Who you are. But it is just a voice, and voices can be listened to or not. And voices can be silenced if one chooses to do so. It is our choice then as to what we want to hear. And when we make the choice for God, we choose the only part of us that's real — the part that lies within us waiting to be re discovered; the part that is the whole.

ON REAL LISTENING

Listen as the stars might listen. Listen and you'll hear the song of all eternal life... the life that always was, and will forever be. Not the life you see with eyes; the life that you can listen to when you are deep in space... deep within yourself where you can hear without a sound the Voice for God. 'Tis not a voice that speaks in tongues; 'tis not a voice that makes a human sound. It is a Voice that speaks to you in absolute completeness of all things you want to know. It is the Voice of knowledge that you hear when deep in space. Do not attempt to draw a picture of this Voice — in words it cannot be. But feel the Voice, and know it's there — telling you that everything you ever wanted in your life is yours... already yours. It is a thrilling Voice, a Voice we all should listen to more often than we do.

On the Ego

ON THE EGO

The ego lives in fear of being demolished. That is why it does its utmost to cause pain and jealousy and anger and sorrow. For without these feelings the ego would have no purpose and no use. And thus it would but fade on into nothingness. The real Self, on the other hand, has not a thing to fear, for it's complete unto itself. It needs nothing from anywhere, for it is love complete. And total love can be or do nothing except extend itself and thus grow ever more beautiful, peaceful, giving and true to the One Who has created it. Battles with the ego are pointless, for they have no meaning except to perpetuate the idle error that the ego thrives on. If you but know this, you will find it easy answering the question: Should I acknowledge the ego, or should I realize it is not real?

ON THE EGO'S ROLE

If we're to be aware of where we're truly headed, then we must put ourselves into the hands of Higher Self — into the hands of spirit that knows so much more than we. Yet we must not ignore the self that seems to be the victim of all circumstance — the ego self. Remember that the ego is not helpful, but it also is not helpless. For though it won't assist you in achieving your true goal, it also won't be helpless in attempting to delay your own advance. When spirit takes completely over, and you're in the hands of All, it's then you can relax and have no fears about the intervention of the ego. For you won't perceive the ego now, and you will be on your way Home. And so don't try to fight the ego; it's a fruitless task. Accept that it is what it is, and simply know its role for now. When you're in conflict, just accept the fact the ego's playing out the part it was created for, and recognize that it is just a role you have decided it will play. And "role" it simply is. Not real. The curtain will come down on it, and then it will be gone... until the time that you decide its next performance is. However, there need never be a "next performance" if you choose as such. And if there isn't, then the ego will for certain be completely "out of work," for it will have no stage on which to play its role. And thus the "drama" that we choose can then be conflict-free. If all this seems completely hypothetical to you, that is because you cannot picture it as possible. It can however be; and if you just believe it can, it will. For though you may believe you do exist within the world that you have made, the truth is you exist, but on a different plane — a level without conflict, without agitation... a level that is moved by love, and love alone.

On Union

ON UNION

Get out beyond the body and remove yourself from war, for there beyond the body there can be no conflicts or resentments. It all is very simple; there is totality of union when one goes beyond the body. There are no boundaries, there are no barriers to joining. It is as though a box of air were poured into another. That is the completeness of the unity... a unity one cannot find except by mind. Ignore the bodies of your world when they might tempt you into conflict. The bodies in your life mean nothing by themselves. They age, they ail, they thrive, they fail; but that which hides behind the body never ages, never fails, never knows a single thought but unity of love. That is Who you are; that is Who we all are. And if you but remind yourself when you are tempted to see otherwise, then you will never know another barrier again.

ON UNION

One *can* experience totality of feeling. And when one does, then union with the All is not just known, but felt. Messages and information that are helpful in removing self-defeating blocks begin to filter through. You see big changes in your love of self, because you now know who you are with much more clarity. There may of course be anguish too; the anguish you may feel results from your attempt to fight the you who won't admit that you are God. But that can certainly be overcome. And then the memories will last, and they'll become a part that's integral to the foundation of your growth... a growth that leads to knowing and to teaching love to everyone you touch.

ON UNION

Don't think you'll ever "see" the light of love, for "visions" are for ego eyes, and not for sight that's real. The truth is that God's love has not a thing to do with sight of eyes. And when you come to know this, you will come to love completely without fear... to love without conditions, and to therefore love yourself and every other being just the same. When there are doubts that cross your mind, you will not have to answer them; you simply need dismiss them. Do this and they're gone! Is not this worth the "price" that one must pay? For what indeed can be the "price" except the full release of fear. Remember that the unexpected's readily at hand when you have stopped expecting it. And that is why it's of importance that we sometimes stop and silently avow, "I am at one with All."

A Story

A STORY

Tell the story of a personality who happened to exist a long, long time ago, and who returned to show the world the truth about the truth. Into the wilderness he'd gone to seek the nature of his inner self. And in the darkness of the forest he had "seen" a light so strong that he was sure he never had seen light before. But this light spoke to him from deep within. It said that brightness and shining glory are some of the manifestations of our true self, but that oft' times what we see has no reality. What's truly real is that which we do feel — not what we see. And when we feel the light of all-encompassing true love then are we next to God. And when he'd learned this so it was pure knowledge, he returned into the outer world, and then began to tell his story — not through words, but through the actions of true love. There were, of course, those who became suspicious of his acts, for *they* knew this behavior was to cover up for something to be hidden. And yet they watched, because they could not help but watch. And what they saw eventually was one who never did get old. And as the others aged and died, the young began to notice that he did not age at all. And thus they knew if they behaved as he, they too would never age. So they began to act his way, until such time as all the generations realized this was the secret that would lead to everlasting life — the way to know one's immortality. And thus the secret truth of truth was learned and lived through total love of all by all.

On Joining

ON JOINING

How can relationships be healed? When the trouble between bodies becomes blocked by cement-like attitudes, a total dissolution is necessary. Man-made tools can chip away at the cement, but the pieces remain shattered and ugly. Only God can dissolve that cement, and if you ask then it shall happen. Give yourself completely to your Higher Self, and then you can know only love. There is no other way. Why block relationships of love when love's the only feeling that is true. What purpose is there holding rigid-like positions? If you but ask yourself this question, you will find there is no purpose, since our only purpose is to love. If you have, or know, a better purpose, speak it loudly to your brothers and thus let them learn your greater truth. Or else be silent, and begin to love your brother in the way that God created you to do.

ON JOINING

I am the Holy Son of God; my function is to teach the world to love, and only can I do this if I know that love completely. To begin with, one must see one's self as sinless; only then can one begin to love one's self. And in that love — that total love — can one extend one's self to all the others if one wants. It is our choice, for either we extend our love or manifest our fear, and in so doing, others feel as do ourselves. The choice seems simple... one leads to peace, the other to distress. Which would you want? The one you choose, of course. So see yourself as one with all the world, and have the world look back at you that way; or see yourself as separate, and all the others will see separately as well. It is entirely up to you; have others see in love, or have others see in fear. Show them the way, and they will join you on your way back Home.

On Healing

ON HEALING

Healing is a state of mind. Healing is a means of affecting the body through the mind-changing process. When one is truly in a state of healing readiness, nothing can stop the change from occurring. To get into that state of readiness, one must have the knowledge that one can be in that state through change of mind. Do not let false perception lull you into states of fear. There is, as you well know nothing to fear. But there may be times when this is not so easy to acknowledge. And at such times just ask yourself "what choice do I prefer — the choice of healing or of fear?" The choice is simple, but it's not so simple to accomplish, for we've programmed part of us to think it can't be done. Deep in your heart there is the knowledge though of what is real and what is not. Just ask for help in reaching for that knowledge so it can become a total part of your own total self. And at such times the time of healing will occur. And you can then forever be forever free from fear.

ON HEALING

To heal is to make true. And healing is the gift of God that lets us know that we're created perfectly, for anything imperfect is a misperception, and each misperception can correct itself as easily as it was made. One only has to have the knowledge, for knowledge breeds the faith that one must show in order to correct mistakes. There's nothing that's mysterious about healing. But with each healing there is almost always found an element of fear that comes directly from the ego self. For if the mind can heal the body, then what power does the body have? And herein lies the basis for the ego's constant drive to show the body real. Just think of all the times when you have suddenly seemed ill. Can you recall the reasons for that illness? There had to be some ego thoughts that let you see your body sick. And then think back and see if being ill did you much good at all. Perhaps it seemed to be of benefit, but any benefit it seemed to have was really none at all. And so it is each time one sees himself as ill. So if you do not wish to play that game again, then reach down to the light in you and let your true Voice speak; and let yourself be healed for good.

On Identity

ON IDENTITY

S tairways leading to a river flowing gently through the caverns of one's mind. There within the darkness one has made, one sees a shaft of light that penetrates the gloom with brilliance far surpassing all the deepest shadows of one's thoughts. You *are* that cavern, and God's light is shining in you now and always. Just turn and you will see that you are bathed in all the brilliance that there ever was. The light is your inheritance — made *of* you and made *for* you. And in that light of love your own salvation lies. Why would you keep from turning to the light? Is everything you cannot see in blackness and in mystery so filled with hopes of better things that you would never even turn to see the Who of Who you really are? What craziness is this? It is the work of ego forces showing you a so-called better way. But once you turn and see the light, you'll know there is but one real way; and you will not turn back!

ON IDENTITY

A lthough we often ask ourselves where we are going and just why, we do not often get the answer that will satisfy us at the time. If you can see yourself as just a mote that's dancing in the light, and know that you're complete unto yourself, and yet so small you are unseen most times, then you will know exactly Who you are — a part of the entire whole. Without that mote the scene appears as incomplete; without your soul, God too is incomplete. For you, as spirit, are God's true creation which, just like the mote, you cannot see except in light. And yet you too are there, as you will always be. Be most aware the answer cannot satisfy you from an ego point of view; but then, an ego you are not. Besides, as spirit your sole purpose is to know precisely Who you are and recognize your goal — to know you don't have any goal except to *know* that you are God and God is you.

ON IDENTITY

Faces in an oblong mirror searching for the power that abides within us all to know the true reality of love. And when we see those faces and can recognize that they belong to all of us, then will we know that form and figure have no substance of their own, but merely represent the force that brings us to the edge of all eternity, waiting for the moment when we dare to take the step that will release us from all pain and guilt. We are in charge; make no mistake of that. And by the "we," we mean that we as individuals must determine that we will see ourselves as truth and as a part of the entire whole. And as an individual who seems to be apart, it's our responsibility to look with new-found eyes and see ourselves exactly as we are. And with that choice we make the dedication to allow ourselves to see that we are not apart at all, but that we are a part. It is the taste of time gone by that causes such confusion if we let it rule our minds. And so we say "not now," "not me," "not us." And know that this alone will be enough to start us on our way again.

ON IDENTITY

E choes that reverberate throughout one's self help tell the story of a billion souls that are but one. Sound waves silently await to face the evil of the ego's stated goal, and with those waves of sound all shadows will become as though disposed of by some strange but potent force. The power of the ego is no match for all the love that's waiting for release from deep within the cloistered room where we are secretly attempting to dispose of it. But who is able to dispose of something not disposable ? And where would one dispose of that which cannot be disposed ? And thus we celebrate the realization that *we* are in control, and that we need not bow to that which sees us dead. And we rejoice that we can know the truth of Who we really are.

On Faith

ON FAITH

Do not concern yourself with matters that have nothing to do with the spirit. Those are out of your control. Just ask for help, and then do as you're guided to and then let go. Don't worry that the things the ego fears will come to pass, for they will only come to pass if you continue dwelling on them and continue giving substance to them. Otherwise the ego is a mere idea — a thought — and nothing more. But if you dwell on it, it will become much more. What then to do with matters of concern?

Faith is the key. Faith and trust in Higher Self that knows alone the answers that will mean the most. When you can trust that Higher Self then you will know the faith that you must have. And with your demonstration of that faith, the world will start to heal itself. So think... is this what you would want? If so, then is your function known.

ON FAITH

Have faith, and you will have whatever you may ask. There is no reason why a child of God should not receive what's rightfully one's own. That's why it never must be thought that there are things that can't be done, for there is nothing that cannot be done. Just let the light of love shine from your heart, and into everybody else's heart. Then, in your eyes, will all be joined... will all be one... will all be *known* to be as one. Just as the trees are meant to grow toward heaven, so is it that one is meant to grow the same, forever reaching for the Light of God until such time as it may be attained. And at that time the world is one. And there will be no other thoughts of other worlds and other ways, because there *are* no other ways.

On Discovery

ON DISCOVERY

To find the Light within, just let your mind go to a far-off space and then return toward where you first began. When you're in touch with the reality that lives beyond perception, then you know what's true and what is special. Nourish the privacy of your inner world, for it leads to the nurturing of the outer. It can soothe and gentle the outer world, but that won't mean it automatically will do so. You must at all times be aware — with the memory of Who you are as guide to you — in order to allow yourself to see the love that always has been there, but which you have refused to regularly see.

ON DISCOVERY

White clouds, white light, the mystery of life pursues us through the world we call eternity. And yet there is no mystery at all, for deep within the clouds, and bright behind the light there dwells the knowledge of the truth of Who we really are. There is no need to draw circuitous circles one within the other trying to reveal the way to peace, the way to open doors. All doors are open if you but straighten out all lines of thought that have been seeing things as circular and mind-confused. There is but one direction, and we all will see it when we choose to open up our hearts. Let not the so-called logic of your ego mind deter you from the only truth there is : the truth that everyone must know that there is but a single goal — the only goal there ever was. Just open up your heart and see within the clouds you've made... open up your heart and fill the world with all the light that lies within. And when you do, the light expands as deeply as the thought we call infinity to touch ourselves and all our Selves and thus to join and share the joyousness of knowing we are one and that we always were. There is no other truth. What could there be when nothing else has any lasting matter to its frame. The only thing eternal is your love, and that has always been and that will always be. So why deny it longer, or refuse to recognize its truth unless you choose denial of the knowledge that is yours. We all have done this much too long; is it not time to choose again, and find that you have never left your Home.

On Choice

ON CHOICE

The time for change has come, and with your change of mind a thousand others are affected and will change as well. Close therefore all the doors that lead nowhere; what you would find behind them are mere maps of yesterday that could not help but lead you wrong. So take the first real step of your own life — the step that leads to now — and feel the strength that will elect the path that leads you Home. There is no other way.

ON CHOICE

There is a world within you that is everything you ever wanted to attain. There is a world within you that no person can attack. The world within holds all the love and peace there ever was or is, and in that world it is your choice to be. It is a simple matter to decide; it is not difficult to make the choice. But you must constantly remind yourself that this is really what you want, for it is much too easy to forget and jump into the world of strife and seeming gain. When it is put to you that it's your choice to make, it may seem terrifying at the very first. But there is no reality to fear of perfect love. And so it is another part of you that's playing on those fears. Is this the way you choose to live ? Who answers "yes" is answering untrue... untrue to that which is the only part of one that's real. So make the choice, and make it every instant of your life. And in that choice your life will always be; and so will all of those you love.

A Story

A STORY

There is a song that is so beautiful that everybody who is born knows the entire melody before they even can begin to speak. Everyone, at one time or another, tries to get inside the melody to try to feel what makes it so hauntingly memorable. But there is no way this can be done, simply because the song is of one piece. It has no beginning or end; it merely is a piece of music... knowingly beautiful music that sings of the joy of all that ever was. Sensing it is senseless to dissect the music, trying to determine if its secret can be learned and therefore duplicated, everyone just sings the song as part of one's inheritance. One does not wonder who has written it, or how it came to be; one merely knows it is a part of self. And yet it's also all of self, for it says wonders to whoever hears it sung. It is the road map Home... it is all things that ever had been learned... it is a song for all to sing until there is no thing called "song" at all. Composed by everyone who ever was, or who will ever be, the song goes on to draw us to such time as time will cease to be.

On Oneness

ON ONENESS

You are the holy son of God who has within you total knowledge of everything that ever is or was, You are complete, because you're one with all the universe. You lack of nothing, and no one you touch lacks anything. Within you is the knowledge to allow that you be anything you choose. You can know *all* if that is what you want, or you can feel there's nothing that you know if that but be your choice. There's nothing that's outside of you that can have any influence on you, because there *is* nothing outside of you. All that you think you do perceive, you do create; and in creating thus, you live with the results that you perceive. Take then the hand of God that always is held out to you; take it because it's yours. And in that joining will you choose to know that we are all the same — that we are each other... that what we felt was separateness was only fear, and that there be no need to ever fear again.

ON THE KNOWLEDGE OF ONENESS

How can one describe the knowledge of perfect oneness? How can one find the words to express a feeling so complete that the feeling must be experienced to be understood? Because there are no words that can describe this knowledge, it does not mean the knowledge is not real. In fact, the closer one comes to the knowledge, and the more that one has touched it, or has bathed in it, or simply lived it, then the more one knows it cannot adequately be described. The knowledge then is simply there for all to experience, as millions have done so already. That doesn't mean, however, that we all can do so now. But it does mean that we have the real potential for experiencing it. So if one asks you what it's like... don't be embarrassed at the lack of words; just point the person in the right direction, and if he is ready, he will go. And then he too will know.

ON ONENESS

The fence posts of life glide by as though in a long lost reverie of motion that was once remembered, but then forgot. It happens to us all as we try to wend our way back Home. We look, we see, but oh how seldom do we know. The fence posts are but markers signaling a temporal past that led us nowhere with such great abandon. And as we think of this, we know the fence cannot go on forever. And on the way to our own destiny there is a time we stop. And look. And see. And know. Beyond the fence is always green and freshly mowed. And at this time we know we can step through the fence, and know that all we then can touch is real. At last. The flowers are me; the grass is you; the earth is us. And you and I are but each other. There is no other way. And as we look beyond the fence, stretching out forever is the grass, laced with flowering shrubs that pass their tender fragrances unto each other... and to us. For we are they, and thus there never more can be a "they."

On Reality

ON REALITY

There is no Spring or Fall or time. There is no way to make your world appear as it really is except within your soul where all is one and there is no day or night. At such time as the universal mind decides to change direction and see things as they really are, then will it no longer see *things*, but only God. There really is no choice to make, for there is no choice at all. There is no here and now except as it may seem to you. And all of that can disappear the instant you decide to stop pretending there is something other than the love of God. Do not allow the world where you reside to influence the you that knows the truth, for that will just delay your journey to your joyful home. There is no joy but in the love of God. And once you have experienced that joy, you'll know it just as you will know that your real home is deep within yourself. Let that be written in your mind to read it over and again until you really know it. And then will it forever be.

ON REALITY

When night is over and the dawn begins to rise, then will Creation be perceived for what it really is: a monument of glory to the grace of all there is and ever was. Do not let anybody tell you otherwise. There may be times when you would doubt all this, but in your heart you know there is but one reality — reality of the eternal truth: that we are one, and that there can be nothing else. Let darkness cast aside its curtain that would hide the truth from all. There is no curtain... there is no darkness... we make it all ourselves, and when we want to make it different, we will use our knowledge to accomplish that. It won't be easy, but if you just do your bit — by learning all the rules that tell you how you can emerge out of the dream — then you'll be playing your full part... and it will be a part of what is certainly a noble whole.

ON WHAT IS REAL

There's no defense that's needed to protect against a feeling that is false, for that which is not real does not in fact exist. When you expose yourself to false attack, and you're defenseless to the same, you are exhibiting the greatest kind of love — the seeing past to the true spirit that forever burns within. And burn it does. Eternally. Our job on earth then is to see that flame burn much more brightly than a pilot light. For that is how we tend to see it. Yet in truth it's burning just as brightly as it can; it knows no other way. We only *think* we know another way, but that is not what's real. Or true. The truth is what we *know* to be within. And with that knowledge we can love the world.

ON REALITY

See the Light within, and know exactly Who you are. The Light that shines from God is part of you, because you are a part of God. Created by Him, loved by Him, and always part of Him. There is no other truth than that. And when you look outside for God or for the means to find the joy and peace you seek, you look into an empty space wherein you can find nothing but the thing you *feel* you want. And by projecting, do you find it in that space. But what in truth is it that you have found when there was nothing there to find? You have, of course, found nothing; but what is so transient it can disappear as readily as it had seemed to come to you. Do not be fooled by such illusions; that is all they are. And that is why you need not at illusion's mercy be, for you have all that's real within you now. So seek it now and you will know the joy and peace of God.

On Dreams

ON DREAMS

What is the meaning of dreams? A dream is the essence of one's hidden being... the very soul of your existence. A dream is the reality of the soul, the life force of all that is meant to be. When one remembers one's dreams, the soul is in contact with the ego. Dreams are a reality... a reality of purpose... a reality of direction. When they are understood, they point the way for you to know the truth of Who you really are; for no matter what the message, the goal is still the same: to find your way back home to God. And dreams not only point the way, but show us where the barricades may be.

ON SLEEP AND DREAMS

To sleep is but to take a step back toward the truth of Who you really are. There is a closeness one can feel for that which is our true reality, and one can feel it deep within the peace of sleep. For when one sleeps one really has the gift of opening one's self to God without the clamor of the world we've made. It is our choice to dream, of course. And dreams can well produce the clamor by themselves. And yet this need not be. The calm and peace of sleep is a first step to feeling what the calm and peace of God is like. We dream because our conscious self does not allow itself to feel that calm and peace. To sleep without the dreams of life would be too threatening to us, and so the clatter of the world invades our nightly aim for peace. It is a safety valve that forces us to dream, for without such, the ego would be dead.

On the Light

ON THE LIGHT

To find the peace we all are seeking, simply ask your Higher Self for help. It will be given, for it is the sanctuary holding everything that's real. Know this, and you will never yearn again for that which is unreal, for you cannot achieve or gain what is not there. Within your heart you'll always know the true direction of your Home. Not somewhere out beyond — but deep within where all your brothers dwell with you. Since on one level you do know exactly Who you are, you do not need reminding... but until such time as you will know on every level, you will have to constantly remind yourself. And as you do, all light will enter both your worlds; the one — in which the Light is always there, but sometimes barely seen; the other, where the Light seems never there, but where you bring the thought to bear so light appears once more. You alone can light the way. Know it, and do it, and live it forever.

ON THE LIGHT

S eek the Light within, and you will find the answer to all questions. Seek the Light within, and know that it's within us all, and that it is the true source of true knowledge. When you find the Light, and let yourself be bathed in it, you'll *know* the meaning of eternal joy. For there's no greater joy than joining with your brother; there is nothing that is more complete. So wait until the time is right, until you reach a sense of peace, and then attempt to join the Light within until it's one with you — until it's one with all.

ON THE LIGHT

To release all fear, know who you are. Know that within the self there burns a Light so blazing in its brightness that it only could be Light from God, your Home. And with this knowledge of the Light that shines within, you then can rest within your heart in knowing that there is no real reality but love... the love of self, the love of God, the love of all. If ever there are times when darkness seems to shroud your vision, you can look within and find the Light that overcomes all traces of the dark, no matter how they seem — if great or small. But it is your own job to find that Light — to keep in mind that it is there, and know that you must ask for help in finding it at times when you might most forget. It then is your decision how you choose to see yourself and all your brothers too. And when you make the choice to see the Light in you, then will you see the love of God and know there are no fears at all.

On Direction

ON DIRECTION

Trails of broken promises that led to golden fields of flowers that were always there but never sniffed or seen. Why do we build such hopeless dreams when dreams are not the answer to the seeming quest we have. Reality of Who and where you are is all the help you need to find your way into the glory of the only goal that we all have. Reality of knowing that we all are there already, and that only by uplifting shades that close our eyes can we begin to see the picture as it really is. There are no golden paths to glory one must seek beyond; the paths are all within. They are but one, and with but one direction: going nowhere, only being where you've always been.

ON DIRECTION

Let the lamp be lit, and it will show the way to all the brightness and the love that shines within us all. It cannot be forsaken when it is a part of you; it cannot be mistaken for a thing which it is not. The lamp that lights our way lights all the paths for all of us to travel on, and when we make the move to venture forward, then will all the light of all the world be shining through each one of us. And with that light comes peace as joyful as the springtime in its most rewarding self. Is this not what each one of us is seeking? Then know it can be yours to have, for it is merely waiting there for you to wake. Keep all sight focused inward, and you'll follow to the goal that God has offered you. Seek not what you can never find, but merely look within and find what you are really of.

ON DIRECTION

The road you want to travel is the way of love... there is no other way. Stop and look at all the signs: they lead to nowhere but detours, because they lead to cul-de-sacs, and then you must return to start anew. The direction is quite clear if only we decide to heed it. Stay on the path, and be not tempted by so called short cuts which really lead you 'round in circles. Remember firstly Who you are, and tell yourself just Where it is you want to go. And with your mind upon your destination, and with the knowledge of exactly Who you are, you're bound to find the most direct route to Where you are inexorably headed. Go in joy, for the road is not as long as you may think. It's even possible to be as short as just a single step. Be not afraid; it takes you Horne where fear was never known.

ON DIRECTION

Go to the far off places of your mind and search for truth that you already know. Go in search of meaning, and come back with life as it is truly known... as it was in the beginning when there wasn't such a thing as "time." Search your heart and you will find the strength to know the oneness of the universe. And when you look for new direction, stop and listen and you will be told which way to go. For deep within us all there is the voice of knowledge. Not acquired, but a knowledge with which we are born. That's why you cannot help but feel the rightness of the path toward God... toward the Light... toward the meaning that you try articulating, but which you are not quite able to express because there are no words that can describe the feelings that you feel.

ON DIRECTION

There is but one direction on the path, so picturing your destination is not difficult to do. But getting there may not be quite as simple, even though the path is clearly marked. For there are lead-offs all along the way, and they are easier to take, it seems, than is the route that is direct. But that is of no matter, for the way is clear and the knowledge one acquires as one moves along the way will, without a doubt, be just as clear. The further down the path one goes, the greater is the knowledge that becomes available, and the greater is the confidence one has that one will reach the ending of the path. Which is where the true beginning really is. So if you're willing to devote the time and energy, then you will know that you too will eventually arrive. And when you are aware of that, there'll be a whole new feeling you will know — a feeling that at last you're going Home.

A Story

A STORY

This is the tale of a new kind of learning, based on the oldest laws of the world. There were three brothers, each of whom was born to the same mother and father. Each was blessed with a loving, caring childhood; each was educated to the best of his ability. And when they each left the home of their birth, they went in different ways. One went to seek his fortune in trade; one went to seek his happiness in power, and one went to seek God. All three accomplished their goals in the eyes of the world. The son who became a merchant became a wealthy man; the son who became a politician became a powerful official; and the son who sought God became himself. There is no moral to this story unless you find a moral in the thought that only the third son had entered Heaven, while the other two would have to try again.

On Recognition

ON RECOGNITION

When the darkness starts to lift, the joy of daylight beams its way through eyes of God and into that pure consciousness of every cell of your own being. The darkness is but yours to lift whenever you decide you've had enough, and that you want to bathe within the light of recognition of exactly Who you are. Waste not the time of growth by seeking reasons for delay; there is no benefit contained therein. Relax and learn to recognize the Who of who you think you are, and then you'll never have to face again a darkness that forever hides the face of peace.

ON RECOGNITION

Take me by the hand and lead me to the land of re discovery. I will gladly go with You when I do realize that You shall lead me to the Home I never left. And this I know is true, as I receive the strength and love that is within Your hand, a strength that I could not believe was mine as well. And as I choose the way I want my life to go, I wonder if indeed I have to go alone, or if the hand that leads me will at all times be right there. For I could not, I feel, return alone. And yet when I arrive, I realize I have returned by my own will. And He Who held my hand is merely there to comfort me and reassure me that the world I then perceive is all I've ever known.

On Perception

ON PERCEPTION

To write of birds and songs and bells is merely writing of perception. Developed through a million years in made-up time, perception waits the single second of a recognition that allows the transformation of the everything into the All. And then we'll know for sure there are no worries that can burden down the backs of all humanity; we'll know for sure they can be lifted any time at will. The beauty of it is, of course, we know it all right now. Yet we don't seem to want to lift the burdens, for we seem to like the game we play. Why not then ask, "How long will we delude ourselves ?" How long until the so called burdens are no longer so perceived? Do you not know? There are no burdens now; there are but dreams. And dreams are made of tinsel that has never seen the light. Dispel those dreams, and you will know the beauty of the world your soul has only known... the only world there is.

ON PERCEPTION

The stars may seem the center of the universe, and yet there is no end. And no beginning too. The world you know does not exist in the one reality of God's eye, which is forever. It is only the way we perceive the world that makes it what we see. Perceive the way you want, but know there is but one reality; know that you are infinitesimal as well as infinite; know the meaning of true love — acting on the knowledge that the world is filled with the fruit of love. And knowing that, we then can know the only meaning we can give to life that's truly meaningful.

ON PERCEPTION

How does one look past the seeming ugliness and violence that is of our own perception ? One only looks past what it is that one decides to see. If you don't wish to see events as tragic, then they obviously now become events that you need not look past. Of course that's not the answer to the question that you ask. To look past those events that seem distressful, one must know, whatever the reality that those events appear to have, that such reality is the epitome of unreality. As an example, an aggression against someone would appear to be just that. But what if you come face to face with him who's called "aggressor?" And what if you can show forgiveness to him — total and complete. The act that had been seen to be "aggressive" then is seen as something else: an act of fear, a plea for help... an act that says "there *is* no ugliness and violence that is real."

ON PERCEPTION

J oy is the absence of darkness. And there is darkness of some kind in everything we do perceive. To find true joy we must go past perception, we must find the truest knowledge of exactly Who we are. And in experiencing this, we'll find and know the God in us. That is what joy is. The touching, feeling, knowing Who we are and Where we must return. To be able to experience the joy of the return is an inherent power that resides within us all. Too often though we don't remember this, and that is why we constantly are seeing all the darkness we have made around ourselves, rather than the light that shines within. Take heart in knowing that it does not have to be the darkness that we constantly perceive. It's up to us to choose a different way, if that indeed is how we really want to see.

On Mystical Experience

ON THE MYSTICAL EXPERIENCE

What is a mystical experience ? An experience that transcends the body and repeats to one's own inner self that the knowledge of the universe is contained within a single cell. There is no knowledge that we do not have within ourselves. The true mystical experience is more than visions, lights and sounds; it is *knowledge*. It is the depth of feeling of completeness that goes far beyond the body, a feeling unlike any purely body-sense that we have ever had. It is the knowledge of the oneness and universality of God. And what is God? It is our inheritance... our creation... our true being... the only being that is real. And in the mystical experience we have the absolute true knowledge of that being. That is why the mystical experience is the most complete experience one can have. Because it encompasses everything there is. Everything that you will ever know or want to know. It is the essence of being... the essence of God.

ON THE MYSTICAL EXPERIENCE

Mystical experiences are memories that seem to float into your mind when you think you have forgotten Who you are. Mystical experiences represent the cornerstone of your true being, since they tell you in dramatic ways that all you think you feel is only part of what you really know. There are all kinds of mystical experiences. They do not have to be considered "spiritual" in nature in order to be part of that real world you never left. There is truth in every mystical experience you have, as well as new found sense in some, in order to expose your mind to something that you need _ to know. The most important thing to do with a mystical experience is to hold it in your consciousness and ask for help in knowing what it's for. The answer that you get will be of infinite real help to you in finding all the inner peace you seek in seeking your way Home.

ON THE MYSTICAL EXPERIENCE

A mystical experience is nothing more than a lesson of love. It is the lesson that we all are one — a lesson that we know, but which we have to keep on giving to ourselves in order to remember. The mystical experience is the purest way of experiencing truth. There are, of course, some other ways, which are at your disposal if you wish to use them. There is the lesson of loving your brother at all times, of seeing no one guilty, of not seeing attack, of not defending yourself, of being one in thought with everyone. These are feelings that you have within you that you could teach every day. The mystical experience merely reinforces truth for you at times when you most need it, and when it will be most helpful for your growth.

On Peace

ON PEACE

"Forever" is the word you use to tell yourself how long it takes before there will be universal peace. The word is incorrectly used, for you already have eternal peace within you now. It's just that you have need to ask for help in bringing it to you for you to feel. It *can* be done, for though you know you know, you still insist on acting in a way that says you don't. From one day to the next you change, however, even though you may not think you do. So be aware of change for that is paramount in letting you allow the peace within to move out of the shadows of your mind.

ON PRAYER AND PEACE

L et there be silence when the world is in its most defensive state. When nations and peoples are un-united, let there be prayers, the only way you have to join together. In prayer there is a goal that's joined that is completely conflict-free. There is a space in which all minds are one without intrusions of the ego self. There can be peace on earth if you decide to find it in your hearts. For peace is love, and love is your inheritance. When bodies are not peaceful it is just because the split mind has decided thus. And when the nations of the world are not at peace, the reason is the same. Stop thinking then of nations, and begin to pray for those who represent the nations of the world. If you can help them heal their minds, they too will know then Who they are, and will find peace themselves. It really is quite simple; many have experienced it happening within themselves, and others can as well... both those who lead and those who follow, for all are all the same.

ON PEACE

With peace, you either feel it or you don't. There's no such thing as "partly peaceful," and that's why the greatest gift that you can give yourself is what we call the peace of God. It is, of course, all yours to give, for God created you in true perfection, and in that perfection lies the total peace of your Creator. Do not, however, simply wait and think that it will come to you; your ego self will never let it come. You must desire to reach down to that one part of you that's real and see the peace you seek is there for you to know. And if you only ask to find the peace of God, you will be answered, and you'll know at last the glory of the only Home that is forever yours.

On Remembering

ON REMEMBERING

Be sure the whole eternal feeling of one's life is met with love and understanding so that nothing can impede the plan for the return. Do not attempt to figure out how such a plan may work, or what it may turn out to be; just work with trying to achieve the plan, for be assured it will be shown to you. Next time you render an opinion of yourself that is not holy, tell yourself "I won't accept that as reality," and you can thus release such feelings of yourself as well as of all others. There is no need to suffer then in any way. Learn to forgive and to release, for what you think you've made has never even been part real. It's like forgiving someone for a thing that was not done, and if not done, how can it hurt in any way? So be at peace; there is no reason not to be. For God is always with you, and the plan is always there. Remember, then... remember to remember, and if you do, you never will forget and will be an example for your brothers who seek peace.

ON REMEMBERING

Where have we been that we are so aware of times and places that are not of us ? What does it mean when we see women masked with veils beside a market square, or tiny birds that search for newts along an unknown water's edge ? They are a part of us somehow. The giant trees that grow, unfettered by a universe that is not civilized... all strange and alien shapes and forms and figures that are brought to our reality in dreams and images. Working in a dimly lighted cellar with a sureness and a certainty not known by me, I wonder what it means. Are these but dreams that have no meaning other than their being? Or do they tell us once again that time is always — neither yesterday nor tomorrow, but always — and that we are all a part of everything that ever is. When you can feel that — with a knowledge that defies all challenge — then do you know the meaning of the universal life.

ON REMEMBERING

When does light shine through to perfect knowledge? When one is able to forget the past and remember one's true Self. When that occurs then will you know the joy of God — the joy completeness brings. There are no easy ways to let go of the past; there are no easy ways at all. It is a matter of determination and of faith. Together they will bring you to that point in space and time that will be unlike anything you have experienced. It is a sense of nothingness — of weightlessness — of freedom to stretch out unto the farthest reaches of the universe. And then beyond. And that is when you'll know the truest meaning of real joy. And love. And God. For they are ever One. So practice lessons God has taught... all lessons based on love. They are reminders of the way to reach your goal.

A Story

A STORY

Once there lived a craftsman who decided to build images of things that were most meaningful to him. He started with the thought, and from the thought came measurements that would begin to shape whatever it was that he had decided to create. And where the basic work was done, he was quite pleased, and yet he wondered what some others possibly might think about his work. There could, he thought, be some who might not like the shape of part, or even of the whole. And so he thought to change it some, First just to please the ones who might like one part differently, and then to please some others who might feel a different way. And when he had completed this, it still looked like the image that had pleased him so, but somehow it was not the same, and did not please him as his first creation had. And yet he feared without the changes he would only please a few; maybe himself alone. And so he set his work for all to see. And some liked it a bit, and some liked it a lot and some did not like it at all. But not one cared for it as he had cared for the original. And so he modified it more, in hope that he could please them all — those whom he thought preferred one thing, and those he thought might want another... till such time as he could not remember what it was he'd first created. And still he pleased no one the way he had originally pleased himself. And so he did the only thing that he could think to do — he reconstructed his creation till the piece was as it was when he had first completed it. For he now realized he couldn't please them all — so why not simply please himself. And when he then displayed his work inside the window of his shop, the people came and marveled as they looked in admiration. For they recognized it was a perfect work that he had made, and they all asked if he would make the same for each of them.

On Many Things

ON CREATION

Long ago when time was but a speck in the imagination, it was not feasible to be anything but that which was. There were no causes and effects. There were no means and ends. There were no whys and fors. The simple truth was that there only was the Truth of the Creator. And in that Truth there lived the blessed means of love and of well being. It was as if today you saw a sunrise over virgin mountains where you stood alone, and where you suddenly became as one with everything you saw or heard. The birds that fly, you flew with; the streams that rush, you flowed with; the trees that stretched to God, you grew with. And in that oneness is the Truth we all must reach. For that is our inheritance, and that is where we surely must find Horne.

ON MEDITATION

There's always time for further meditation. Then let the night air's thoughts sweep over you like warm waves from a gentle sea. And bathe yourself in what those thoughts may be. For in them you may find some answers to some questions you may or may not know you have. When passively you dwell on them, then will you grow and learn and start becoming more attuned to everything about yourself that's real. And that's a goal to really strive for — to attune yourself unto yourself, your real and inner self... to let yourself feel what the real you happens to be all about.

ON PURPOSE

What is the answer? The answer and the question are the same, because there really are no questions, and there only is one answer: to hear the Voice of God and know the one reality of God is all there really is. There are, of course, other seeming realities; there are many. But they are temporal manifestations to keep our egos from coming to grips with the only purpose that there is: to know that we reside in God. When you remove all doubts of this, when you're aware this knowledge is complete, then you have all the knowledge that there ever was. Don't be concerned why others may not seem to want to manifest true love. Concern yourself with only your own self, and you will see that others will be traveling the path along with you. They must. Because without you they are lost, and no one wishes to be lost.

ON ATTAINING JOY

What is it that you really seek? A job that pays you more ? A life that seeks more pleasure? Or a heart that's filled with joy? When one can answer that from deep within one's inner Self, the goal of one's existence on this plane becomes more certain, and the purpose of one's life becomes more sure. For what can fill your heart with joy except the only love there ever was — the love that God created... the love that one beholds in all whom God would call His own. Can you but think of what your heart would feel if you could feel at all times such a lovingness as this? Where would there be the room for envy and for jealousy and hate ? These words would not exist. Is this an unreal dream of which we speak? Or is the dream we live the only unreality? If we would only take the step to see there is no pain, no fear, no loss, we then would know the only meaning joy can ever have.

ON THOUGHT

Deep is the night that comes when the face of the earth is mixed with unreal thoughts. The light of God may be eternal, but do you know it's shining if you cannot see it shine? Behind that thought is why the world must learn to live with love, for love is light. Remember that, and you will *know* that *you* are God, and that there is no other way of thought. It may sound overly simplistic, but it's not. For God is quite a simple thought; the thought of love within the hearts of all.

ON TIME

Time is the adversary of reality. It makes a mockery of all that is God-given, for time can never be anything but what man makes of it. What God gives is timeless and eternal; what God gives is love. What can time make of love except a complete distortion that can bring as great a gift of pain as it can of joy. This is not what God meant love to be used for. God's love is only joyful, and when you experience that love outside the limits of time, then do you know the truest, only meaning that it has. Time was made by beings when they thought they could out-think the Mind of God, which thought itself is but insanity. Since time is temporal, then love experienced within the context of time is temporal as well. And this too is insane itself. God does not create what is but temporal, but only what is known to be eternal. Think then which kind of love you wish to feel. It is your choice — the choice for time and space, or the choice for ever. Taste eternal love, and know the joy of joining... the oneness that can only come in knowing that true love is not dependent on a rendezvous in time, but that in truth it always is, wherever you may think you are. For what indeed is perfect love, but simply knowledge that you *are* your brother, and that he is you. And knowledge does not make appointments to be kept or not at varied places and at varied times. Knowledge simply is; and knowledge such as that you carry with you even as your body moves from place to place. It does not stay behind nor move ahead to wait for your arrival at some pre-determined place. That is the basis for your knowing Who you are, and Who all others are as well. Bring that knowledge to your conscious self, and constantly remind yourself that love is yours and love is you. In such a way you will of course love all the world, and all the world will then love you.

ON GROWTH

How do I grow? How many ways are there to let loose and expand? There is really only one way to grow, and that is through love. Through total acceptance of all your brothers and sisters. Then will you know the world is part of you, and you are all the world. In comfort will this happen. In comfort and in joy. For the exhilaration of total love and acceptance leaves nothing else to be desired. If this is so then it is easy for us all to understand the reason why the world must strive for this. And yet the ego will not let it be, and helps deny the truth we know is so. It knows that if there's nothing else to strive to get, there would be no more reason to go on. And that is quite correct. No reason to continue *in this form*. We would go on to higher forms though, where those even greater truths would then be learned and be accepted and so on and on to Home.

ON GUILT

Guilt is the summing up of all the ego's defenses in order to let you know the ego's real. By allowing you to feel the brunt of its attack, guilt makes you think that you're a prisoner — that you can never be completely free. You must then be alert to all the dangers put before you by the ego mind. It is insane to think that guilt can be of any use to you; and what could you have done that would allow such guilt to even be? A word? A look? A thought? You merely have been taught that they spell guilt. But ego teaching is not real. Just recognize this truth, and live then in an atmosphere of purity and light that leads to even broader and to even brighter light till all you ever see or know or feel is total oneness of the all. For being one is being love, and in that being you must know exactly Who you are. In working towards this goal, do not let guilt allow itself to place its ugly face before your path. Dismiss what seems reality, for it is but a trick your mind has played, and you are not in any way obliged to play the game.

ON CONSCIOUSNESS

Where is my consciousness? Where is the part of me that knows the all that ever was ? Where did we hide it, hiding all its grace and beauty 'neath the depths of matter that don't matter? Why can we only touch our true reality at fleeting moments only giving us a taste of Who we really are? Why just odd moments out of an entire life? Perhaps to show us that "odd moments" are the only time there really is... that all the rest is space between reality of God and reality of Who we are, which really are the same. The space then is "between" what can't be separate, and thus the space itself cannot exist at all. Touch that moment of consciousness and you know Who you are; touch it and it becomes the goal you ever seek. And if we know the truth of that, then why do we not touch it over and yet over once again till all the "spaces" in between shrink down to nothingness. Is our ego so all potent as to thus prevent our reaching what we never have let go ? It seems a frightening thought, but one that need produce no fear, for that which has no real reality can certainly produce no fears. Just ask to know and touch your Self, and it will be. More often than before... more often and more often till you are at Home at last.

ON COMMUNICATION

S end forth the words that come by Light, and see the way the world can change. And with the stimulus of thoughts from God there comes the certainty of knowledge that does live within us all. Do not be loath to send the words; there is no higher form of love than sharing love. And with this sharing comes more love than one might possibly expect. Be your own guide, though not alone, and you will know how peaceful and how right your own direction is. So do as you are led to do. It is a matter that will bring the joy of recognition to untold numbers, and will help you find your way to God in even brighter ways.

ON FORGIVENESS

Tell not the story of forgiveness if you do not live it. By living it, you then do tell it. As we have said before, the more it's told the more it is received. Forgiveness is the holding of your brother in complete and total innocence. It's loving that's complete, and acceptance of your brother and of all he does or ever will do. There are no conditions you attach to true forgiveness; you either forgive, or your ego does not. In living with this concept in your mind, you realize there can be no reward for you except the gift of oneness. So try to reach that point, and feel the peace that comes as you approach your final goal.

ON JEALOUSY

Jealousy is the voice of the ego proclaiming that there is no justice in the ways of God. "Would God have put on earth another soul to torment his brother with his actions of defiance?" asks the ego. And when one answers loudly, "no," the end result must be there is no God. But God is perfect love and nothing more, because there is no more. Then why do feelings we call "jealousy" exist? It is an ego trick; there are no jealous feelings that a child of God can feel, for how can one be jealous of one's self? We all are one, and in that oneness we are all alike. Release the body from your thoughts; it is not real at all. Remember only love, for that is what you are. And in that lovingness of minds that join, we are but one and thus there is no feeling for your brother but the feeling of acceptance and of joy.

ON SENSES

Beyond the senses are the golden rays of everlasting light which shine through us continually. Beyond the senses is the one and only truth that is the keystone of all knowledge. Beyond the senses are the other senses we must reach in order to acknowledge there is knowledge that can lead us to the only peace there is. And when we reach that knowledge then we know we've done so through the senses that are ours, but not through senses we are used to calling on. There are many senses past the five we speak of ordinarily, and we can use them all to find and feel the one perception... that which is our natural inheritance. Once we do find it, we then hold that knowledge, and we then can recognize that we are closer to our goal.

ON PRIORITIES

Make a list of all the things that seem so meaningful to you. And then begin eliminating from the list, and see if anything is really lost. There's nothing that is meaningful, you'll find, except the truest form of love. And when you realize this truth, you'll realize that all your values have been misconceived. And this will be of great importance in your reaching toward your goal of peace and happiness. For moments of real joy that we experience are hard to come by without feelings of true love. That's why you're asked to re assess your values and determine what it is you really want. That way you can decide how best to go about achieving that which you so eagerly desire to achieve. There is no secret to it; there only is the difficulty of un-learning all you've learned these many years. But it is able to be done, and it will be well worth it too, for you will find a new joy when you do.

ON DOUBTING

When doubts of God appear, it is the function of the mind to overcome those doubts with the true knowledge that God is in us all. For where else could God be? It is for all of us to work toward the dissemination of this knowledge, for only in this way can the world of man be truly healed and the World of God be acknowledged as It truly is. There will be times when it will seem the journey is too long. But do not worry over that. There really is no journey, for you are already there.

ON BEING HOME

Certain is the course of all that's loving in the one reality... certain is the thought that all will find the way to God, the way that none has ever left. When one believes a gift is lost, but in reality it has not been, then what could possibly impede the use of such a gift when one at last does recognize it's still a part of him.

The same is true of knowing Who you are. You do already know the answer, but you seem completely unaware of this, and so you wait and wonder when the answer will appear to you, as well as how and where it will appear. Do not look *out* to find the peace that knowledge brings, for all the knowledge that you need dwells deep within your Self. It merely takes a willingness and self-determination to uncover it. And then you'll know, when you've shut down the clatter of the world you've made, and opened up your heart to God. Within the peace of meditation will you feel your Home, and once you have that feeling you will know you have no place to go — that you are there already, and that you have always been.

ON HEAVEN

Heaven is the quest of the holy. And in truth since all of us are holy, Heaven is our universal goal. And yet how many will acknowledge this? For to acknowledge it would be a frightening thing. To feel that what we have not yet achieved is holy is too terrifying for most people to confront. And yet if you approach the thought with knowledge that Heaven has already been achieved (since we have never left) then all we have to do is find that knowledge, and uncover all the peace and beauty that has always been not just a part of us, but *all* of us that's real. Look not outside for help to know you are a part of Heaven; look within and know the Who of who you really are.

ON BEING PREPARED

B eing prepared for anything means only being ready within yourself... being peaceful within yourself. If you're at peace within yourself you are prepared for anything that is perceived. Don't fret if you don't know what's coming next; it doesn't matter, for every lesson is the same: to learn to love all souls as one. There are no real dramatic moments in this life we make; they're merely steps to show the way to God. Some may seem more momentous than some others may, but they are really not. For love that is complete and true, no matter how it's manifest, can not be more or less important. It just is.

ON HEALING THE WORLD

When the time is right for healing of the world, the world will surely know it. Until that time it's up to each of us to do our best in trying to get to the point where healing can take place. And when that time occurs, there'll be a joyous transformation of the ego self that spent its life denying love. This transformation leads to feelings that we all have hidden deep within our memories. And it's our job right now to bring forth from those memories the feelings which we speak about. For no one can deny that love's completeness, be it felt, will melt away all else, and will then take the place of the illusion that was never really there. That's why it's so important to work toward the feelings that we speak so often of. For who can doubt the beauty and perfection of those feelings? Only those who fear surrendering the known to the unknown. But they should surely know there's no such thing as the "unknown." There's only the un-knowing.

ON HOLINESS

To feel holy is to feel whole. Nothing is lacking when *you* know you are the perfect child of God. So why won't everyone begin to strive for that? Because the ego makes it difficult. If one feels wholly holy, what then happens to the ego? It has no function any more, and so it will dissolve. Is it any wonder therefore that the thought of feeling holy makes us feel that we're afraid? For we would then be giving up all painful thoughts that we so treasure. Holy people see no suffering, for they perceive it not. So learn to look for holiness that is within you at all times; it's there just wanting to be found.

ON VISION

Take the Path, and feel the very essence that it holds for you... the beauty and the joy. Strip away the layers of your learning so that you can bathe within the glow of everlasting love. Become a part of universal truths... become a knowing part. The key, of course, is knowing what we've always been. There is no other way to understand the way the world is made. You know — all know — there is no logic to the world as seen through ego's eyes, and so why fight it any longer. Open up your eyes and see what always has been there to see. Open up your eyes and watch all others' eyes begin to open up to you. And each of you will then begin to recognize the power of the only truth there is.

ON HAPPINESS

Happiness is the forgetting of pain. It is the forgetting of all things seemingly ugly as well as all things beautiful. For happiness is from the Self within; it can't come from without. Now let us see why many find that happiness seems difficult to reach. The joy of life is deep within us, and we hide it in so many different ways. To start, enumerate the ways, and then decide you will release not one, but all of them. If you desire, you can disallow the presence of all pain and anguish, and let real joy enter to proclaim that you are, and always have been, love. And so have all of those around you. That is when you know the world is one, and happiness is joy forever yours.

ON SICKNESS

Sickness is a way of leaving the God-part of us to Itself, and telling the world that we are here. It is an ego tool, just as are all manifestations of the ego. Do not despair of an illness, merely see it for what it is, and remember Who you are. In doing so, the sickness loses meaning and becomes an unreal dream and then dissolves in deep dismay.

ON PERFECTION

There is no help that any child of God does really need, for "help" implies that one is lacking something that one needs, and not a single child of God is lacking anything. The only lack the child of God would seem to have is lack of knowledge that one really is complete and pure and total love. And this apparent lack is just another ego trick to try to disinherit one from God. The ego tries to tell you that you're missing many things, but listen to the only part of you that's real, and you will know the only truth there is... that you are perfect in the only way that God could possibly create. And that this knowledge can direct you to the Home that you have never left if you will but allow this knowledge in to your awareness of what's truly real.

ON WHAT IS MEANINGFUL

L et it be known that all of life is meant for love... that the secret of loving is *knowing* Who you are — and that there is nothing between us. No barriers. No walls. No structures to restrain the bountiful feeling of one to all. All there is to life is learning... learning how to let go of the seemingly important things we have been told are part of any structure for success. But success and "successful living" are two different things. "Successful living" means you always know just who you are... that you're a Child of God, and that you are the same as everybody else. In. knowing so, you will of course eliminate all barriers within your life; you will be open and all-giving and you'll know the joy of oneness that bespeaks the joy of love. That is where "successful living" starts. And where it ends is in the arms of God. From whence we come. From whence we are.

ON HIGHER SELF

When you hear the Voice for God, you will be *sure* you heard it, and you'll never try again to solve a problem by yourself. Listen for the Voice for God; it is with you eternally, and in its warmth and love you'll feel a safety and a bliss you never knew were there. There is no reason not to ask for help of Higher Self, for It is you, and It would have you suffer not an instant longer. So take the step that is affirmative; be one with God, and you will ever be with Him, and always know exactly Who you are.